The Tudors

Retold by Theatre Workshop

Written by Brian Twiddy And Yvonne Peacock

Foreword

Brian and Yvonne are both professional actors with a fascination for history, and a commitment to working with children. They founded a touring Theatre Company. *'Theatre Workshop'* in 1991, with help from The Prince's Trust, in order to encourage children to discover history through drama, and to learn about drama through history. *'Theatre Workshop'* now travels to Primary schools all over the country presenting workshops and plays, as well as writing and adapting stories for schools.

They are always pleased to hear from old friends and new, or to answer questions about themselves and their work, so please feel free to contact them at their E-mail address, which is theatrew@globalnet.co.uk.

Acknowledgements

© Key Curriculum Publications Ltd., 1999 on behalf of the authors Brian Twiddy and Yvonne Peacock

All rights reserved. The copyright of all materials in this book remains the property of the publisher. No part of this publication may be reproduced or transmitted by photocopier or any other means. All requests for reproduction and other rights must be sent in writing to:

Key Curriculum Publications Ltd., P.O. Box 293, Hemel Hempstead. HP2 7WD. UK.
email: editorial@keycurriculum.com

The only copies that may be made without reference to the publisher are of those pages marked 'COPIABLE' providing that they are for the sole use of the students taught by the person or school buying the publication. Copies may not be made available to other schools or individuals. Copies may not be used to form all or any part of any other publication.

ISBN 1-90236-186-5

Contents

Fact File	4
Helpful Hints	5
Simple Scenery	5
Costume Design	6

The Plays

Henry VII	8
The Season of the King (Henry VIII and His Six Wives)	21
Mary I Takes The Throne	35
A Husband For The Queen	47

Fact File

THE TUDORS

Henry VII – Elizabeth of York

Arthur (died 1502)   Henry(VIII)   Margaret   Mary

Catherine of Aragon — Mary I
Anne Boleyn — Elizabeth I
Jane Seymour — Edward VI
Anne of Cleves
Catherine Howard
Katherine Parr

The Tudor Kings and Queens

Henry VII 1485 – 1509

Henry VIII 1509 – 1547

Edward VI 1547 – 1553

Lady Jane Grey – 9 days in 1553

Mary I   1553 – 1558

Elizabeth I 1558 - 1603

The Tudor period began on the 22nd August 1485 when Henry Tudor from the House of Lancaster finally defeated Richard III from the House of York in a spectacular battle at Bosworth.

Even after this great battle, the feuding continued until Henry Tudor married Elizabeth of York in 1487. This united the Red Rose from the House of Lancaster with the White Rose from the House of York and the Tudor Rose was created.

Henry Tudor had fought a long 'War of the Roses', which had cost not only men's lives but also a great deal of money. He was in need of financial security and so he taxed and fined his loyal subjects whenever he could do so. His money chest swelled over his reign. Little did he know that his second son Henry was to spend it all in his first year as the King of England.

Henry Tudor died in 1509 leaving the throne to Henry VIII. What would have happened if his first son, Arthur, had not died in 1502?

Henry VIII married six times in his quest for a strong heir. When he died in 1547, he had two daughters, Mary and Elizabeth, and his only son Edward. On his father's death Edward became the king of England when he was only nine years old but, being prone to illness, he died six years later, aged fifteen.

Edward VI was followed onto the throne by his half sister Mary I and then by Queen Elizabeth I, known as 'Elizabeth the Great'. Elizabeth I was the last of the Tudor monarchs and also the longest on the throne, as she ruled, during what has become known as 'The Golden Age', for forty five years.

'Helpful Hints'

The plays can be used in a variety of ways, for example, Assembly performances, OFSTED Inspections, open days, also for literacy hour or a class project.

The plays are designed for pupils to add or remove characters and dialogue, in order to give everyone a role, or to add new stage directions. In short, we would encourage pupils to be creative with, rather than bound by each play.

The playlets may be used as an introduction to drama. Instead of acting out the scenes, simply change them into a 'Frozen Picture' or 'Tableau'. After reading the play, groups of eight to ten children create a 'Frozen picture' that summarises the story.

These pictures may then be presented to an audience with a narrator briefly telling the story. The audience then guess who the characters in the picture are. This technique may be advanced by the actors miming their parts, and finally the text is added to create the play.

Not all children want a speaking role, so there are non-speaking parts for those who wish to be a part of the production, without the pressure of delivering lines.

Simple Scenery Idea

Cover the wall with a white sheet, or white wallpaper, with a large Tudor rose in the centre and a red border. A chair could be covered with red and black cloth to make a throne. To add further atmosphere have Tudor music playing live or on tape.

The Tudor Rose

Children's Costume design

There is no need to hire costumes. The following is a way for all members of the cast to wear a simple but effective costume.

1. Black top. Polo neck if possible but a T-shirt or Vest will do as well.

2. Black tights, leggings or trousers.

3. Black socks and pumps.

4. Ruff

5. Cloak.

Cloaks vary depending on the part the pupil is playing. Black cloaks for guards or servants. Coloured cloaks for royalty etc. if a peasant, then a rough or dirty cloak, and so on.

Instruction for making a cloak:

- Fabric any colour. (Approx. 50cm in width and 1 metre in length.)
- 50cm of rufflette tape.
- Ribbon, Tape or string for fastening.

Sew the rufflette curtain tape to the top of the piece of fabric (50 cm width). Pull the strings either end of rufflette and tie off at each end. Attach tape, ribbon or string to the ends of the rufflette and use this to fasten the cloak. Decorate the cloak with gems, ribbons, a coat of arms, or glitter if required.

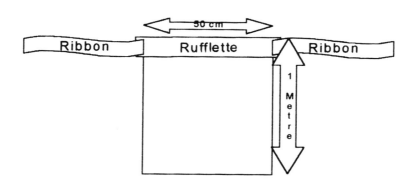

© Key Curriculum Publications   COPIABLE PAGE

Instruction to make a Ruff.

- Thin card.
- Scissors.
- Pencil.
- Tape measure.
- Dinner plate or round object.
- A pin.
- A ruler.

Place the plate onto the card and draw a circle. (Do this twice).

Measure around the neck and add 2 cm, cut a piece of string to one third of the resulting length.

Loop the string around a pencil and fix the ends to the centre of the card circles with a pin. Draw a circle with the pencil, then cut around the line to remove the centre.

Measure the width of the cardboard rings, and then cut a strip of card to the same width.

Fold the strip of card into pleats and join the two ends together forming a ring.

Glue this pleated ring onto one of the cardboard circles, and then glue the other circle on top.

To put the Ruff on, simply cut through one side and twist it open. Decorate your ruff, BEFORE you glue.

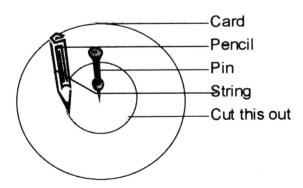

Henry VII
and The Monkey

Cast list:

King Henry VII

Elizabeth of York

Ladies in Waiting (two, or more if required)

Guards (six, or more if required)

Servant (one, or more if required)

Chancellor

Monkey

Prince Arthur

Prince Henry

Princess Margaret (non speaking)

Princess Mary (non speaking)

Henry VII and the Monkey

Scene:
The thrown room of King Henry VII. King Henry the seventh and Elizabeth of York are sitting at a large table looking at a pile of bills in front of them. There are guards positioned around the room and either side of them there is a servant, who is offering Henry and Elizabeth some food from a tray.

Henry VII.
Bills, bills, bills. Where am I going to get the money to pay them all? What about your family Elizabeth?

Elizabeth of York.
Husband, my family in York doesn't have any. All there money was spent paying for the war of the Roses, which you won.

Henry VII.
I know I did, that's how I came to be the king, and now that I am Henry the seventh King of England, everybody comes to me for money. Where's my chancellor?

Guard 1.
Call the chancellor.

Guard 2.
Call the chancellor.

(Enter the Chancellor.)

Chancellor.
Yes my Lord.

Henry VII.
How much money do I have?

Henry VII and the Monkey

Chancellor.
  I don't know sire.

Henry VII.
  You don't know! You're the Chancellor, you should know. What do I pay you for?

Elizabeth of York.
  But you haven't paid him Henry.

Henry VII.
  Haven't I, why ever not?

Elizabeth of York.
  Because there isn't any money.

Henry VII.
  There should be, I know the army costs a lot and the staff, food for everyone, even my pet monkey. You, servant *(Points to the servant on his right.)* go and get some nuts for the monkey. (Exit servant.) Then there's your clothes and all the other things, but what about money coming in?

Chancellor..
  There isn't any money coming in.

Henry VII.
  Then we will have to do something about that. We'll make a law that says everyone in the country has to pay taxes to me.

Chancellor.
  They won't like that sire.

Henry VII and the Monkey

Henry VII.
I don't care what they like. I'm the king, and what I say goes.

Chancellor.
Yes sire.

Henry VII.
And go and get me a big book. I want to write down all the money that I spend, and all the money that is paid to me in taxes. Then I will add them all up and the answer will tell me how much money I've got.

Chancellor.
Yes sire. At once. *(To Guard 1.)* Go and buy a big book.

Guard 1.
(Shouts to Guard 2.) Go and buy a big book.

Guard 2.
(Shouts to Guard 3.) Go and buy a big book.

Guard 3.
(Shouts to Guard 4.) Go and buy a big book.

Guard 4.
(Shouts to Guard 5.) Go and buy a big book.

Guard 5.
(Shouts off stage.) Oi! *(Enter Guard 6. Shouts to Guard 6.)* Go and buy a big book. *(Guard 6 runs off stage and straightaway runs back on stage with a big book.)*

Guard 6.
(The guard is out of breath.) The King's big book.

Henry VII and the Monkey

Guard 5.
　The King's big book.

Guard 4.
　The King's big book.

Guard 3.
　The King's big book.

Guard 2.
　The King's big book.

Guard 1.
　The King's big book.

Chancellor.
　The big book Sire.

Henry VII.
　Thank you. You may go.

Chancellor.
　(Aside.) You old misery guts. *(Exit.)*

Henry VII.
　What was that?

Guard 1.
　I didn't hear anything sire.

Guard 2.
　I didn't hear anything sire.

Henry VII and the Monkey

Guard 3.
I didn't hear anything sire.

Guard 4.
I didn't hear anything sire.

Henry VII.
Well I did. I'll write it down in the back of this book to remind me. *(Writes it down in the book.)*

(Exit King Henry VII with the book. Accompanied by Elizabeth of York with her Ladies in waiting, the servants and Guards 5 and 6.)

Guard 5.
(Shouts.) Make way for the King. *(Exit.)*

Guard 6.
(Shouts.) Make way for the King. *(Exit.)*

Guard 1.
(Shouts.) Make way for the King.

Guard 2.
(Shouts.) Make way for the King.

Guard 3.
(Shouts.) Make way for the King.

Guard 4.
(Shouts.) Make way for the... Oh he's gone.

Guard 1.
At last, I thought he'd never go.

Henry VII and the Monkey

(King Henry VII looks back from the edge of the stage and scribbles something in the book.)

Guard 2.
Careful. He's writing everything you say down in that book.

Guard 3.
We'd all better be careful from now on.

Guard 4.
Come on we've got work to do. We have to practise our marching.

Guard 1.
And feed the monkey.

Guard 2.
And saluting.

Guard 3.
We've got to polish our spears.

Guard 4.
And feed the monkey.

Guard 1.
I said that.

Guard 2.
What monkey?

Guard 4.
The king has a pet monkey, and we have to look after it.

Henry VII and the Monkey

Guard 1.
> I'll go and get it.

Guard 3.
> I'll get something for it to eat.

(Exit Guards 1 and 3.)

Guard 2.
> What does it eat?

Guard 4.
> Nuts !

Guard 2.
Don't be horrible, I only asked.

Guard 4.
> No you don't understand. It eats nuts, and apples and pears, and cakes, and anything really.

(Enter Guards 1 and 3 with the monkey.)

Guard 1.
> That monkey is a little monster. It's torn my tights.

Guard 3.
> And my shirt.

Guard 1.
It destroys everything.

Guard 3.
> It's no joke you know, this palace is so cold and draughty.

Henry VII and the Monkey

Guard 1.

You don't want that wind whistling around torn tights I can tell you.

Guard 3.

We had an awful job catching it, it keeps getting away.

Guard 4.

Quick it's getting away again.

(The monkey escapes, runs around the stage as the guards chase it. The monkey runs off stage, followed by the guards. The monkey returns straightaway carrying the big book, followed by the guards.)

Guard 1.

Quick, it has the King's big book.

Guard 3.

Get it.

Guard 4.

You get it.

Guard 1.

Not me, I haven't got another pair of tights.

Guard 2.

Wait a minute.

Guards 1, 3 and 4.

What?

Guard 2.

Why don't we just leave it?

Henry VII and the Monkey

Guard 4.
But we'll be in terrible trouble.

Guard 2.
No we won't. Listen. If we just go and leave it, lock the door so that it can't escape, then with a bit of luck the whole book will be torn up into little pieces. Then all the things that King Henry VII has written in it, will be lost forever.

Guard 1.
Yes, and no-one will know who let the monkey have the book.

Guard 3.
Maybe he'll blame someone else.

Guard 4.
Like his two sons, Prince Arthur and Prince Henry.

Guard 2.
That's right.

Guard 3.
Come on then, what are we waiting for.

(Exit the four guards, making sure that they lock the door behind them. The monkey then tears the book into tiny pieces.)

Henry VII.
(Henry VII is heard off stage saying.) Where's my big book?

Elizabeth of York.
(Elizabeth of York is heard off stage saying.) It must be where you left it dear.

Henry VII and the Monkey

(King Henry VII opens the door and enters, followed by Elizabeth of York, the Ladies in waiting and Guards 5 and 6.)

Henry VII.
What's this? Who put that monkey in here? Where's my book? Look at all this mess. I haven't seen a mess like this since the battle of Bosworth. Arthur! Henry! Come here at once.

(The Ladies in waiting point at the mess and start giggling, Elizabeth of York is also trying to keep a straight face. The Guards 5 and 6 stand to attention and pretend not to notice the mess.)

Elizabeth of York.
(Elizabeth of York turns to the Ladies in waiting and tells them to.) Sssshhh *(Enter the two princes Arthur and Henry, quickly followed by their sisters.)*

Prince Arthur.
Yes father.

Prince Henry.
What's happened.?

Henry VII.
You know very well what has happened. You let the monkey out and it has destroyed my big book.

Prince Arthur.
No we didn't father.

Prince Henry.
Anyway, we weren't even here. Besides, you can get another silly old book whenever you want.

Henry VII and the Monkey

Henry VII.
No. That's it. I will not get another book just so that a monkey can eat it.

Elizabeth of York.
Henry, I've just had an idea. *(She whispers in his ear.)*

Henry VII.
As for you two, I know how I can keep you out of trouble, and get some more money at the same time.

Prince Henry.
We didn't do anything.

Prince Arthur.
How father?

Henry VII.
You Arthur, are going to get married. There's a very rich Spanish Princess called Catherine. From a place called Aragon. She'll sort you out.

Prince Arthur.
No father, please, I'm too young.

Henry VII.
Come along, the pair of you.

(Enter Servant.)

Servant.
Your nuts your majesty!

Henry VII and the Monkey

Henry VII.
How dare you!

Servant.
(Shows his majesty a bag of nuts.) For the monkey sire.

(Exit Henry VII and Elizabeth of York. Followed by the two princes, Arthur protesting loudly, and young Henry laughing.)

Guard 5.
(Shouts.) Make way for the King. *(Exit.)*

Guard 6.
(Shouts.) Make way for the King. *(Exit.)*

(Exit the two princesses giving the monkey some nuts, accompanied by the servant.)

THE END

The Season of The King
Henry VIII and His Six Wives

Cast List:

Catherine of Aragon/Or Portrait of her

6 Guards

Henry VIII

Anne Boleyn

Jane Seymour

Anne of Cleves

Catherine Howard

Catherine Parr

Town Crier

Peasant and Voice off stage.

The Season of The King

Scene 1:

Inside the palace of King Henry the Eighth, we see a long corridor. There are six guards standing side by side, facing the audience, between Guards 1 and 2 and Guards 5 and 6 there is a table. The audience can see a portrait of Catherine of Aragon centre stage between Guards 3 and 4. (This is either an actress holding up a picture frame in front of herself or a portrait of her, hanging from the palace wall.)

(A peasant enters, he is carrying a placard, which reads '1533' he walks across the stage and exits.)

1st Guard.
What a life. Party, party, party.

2nd Guard.
You're lucky, I have to stay home and look after my mum.

3rd Guard.
Where's the party?

4th Guard.
There isn't a party.

3rd Guard.
Is it someone's birthday?

5th Guard.
It's my wife's Birthday.

1st Guard.
Nobody's having a party! I was just saying, when Henry VIII, was married to her... *(Points to the picture of Catherine of Aragon.)*

The Season of The King

2nd Guard.
　Catherine of Aragon.

1st Guard.
　Yes... It was party, party, party.

3rd Guard.
　It all finished in divorce though.

4th Guard.
　All because the king wanted a son.

5th Guard.
　I'm getting a divorce.

6th Guard.
　Attention! Make way for the King.

(The guards stand to attention.)

(Enter King Henry VIII with Anne Boleyn from stage left. They walk across the stage arm in arm.)

Henry VIII.
　And of course my dear, I've always admired you.

Anne Boleyn.
　Ooh your Majesty, you are a one. Of course, I'll marry You.

(Exit King Henry VIII and Anne Boleyn to stage right.)

6th Guard.
　At ease! *(The guards all relax again.)*

The Season of The King

1st Guard.
That marriage will never last.

4th Guard.
His majesty and Anne Boleyn.

2nd Guard.
My mum says she'll give it three years. She's always bossing him about.

5th Guard.
My wife bosses me about.

Voice from offstage.
Oi!

3rd Guard.
(Looks off stage.) Eh up, what's going on out there.

(Peasant enters carrying the placard, which now reads "1536", he walks across the stage and exits.)

(1st Guard goes off stage and brings out Anne Boleyn with her head covered; she kneels at the table positioned between Guards 1 and 2 and rests her chin on the top of the table.)

1st Guard.
This has been delivered. *(He removes the cloth to reveal Anne Boleyn's head.) (He turns to Guard 2.)* Looks like your mum was right. It's Anne Boleyn.

2nd Guard.
My mum says that they chopped her head right off.

The Season of The King

5th Guard.
My wife had her head chopped off you know.

1st Guard.
No she didn't.

5th Guard.
Well she nearly did.

3rd Guard.
(Points to Anne Boleyn.) She couldn't have a son in the end.

4th Guard.
Just a princess called Elizabeth.

5th Guard.
I've got a daughter called Elizabeth.

6th Guard.
Attention! Make way for the King and the new Queen.

(Enter King Henry VIII with Jane Seymour from stage right. They walk across the stage arm in arm.)

Henry VIII.
This is great news Jane.

Jane Seymour.
Yes your Majesty and I'm sure my baby will be a boy.

(Exit King Henry VIII and Jane Seymour stage left.)

The Season of The King

6th Guard.
At ease! *(The guards relax.)*

1st Guard.
She didn't look well.

2nd Guard.
Who Jane Seymour? No and that's his third wife. My mum says she'll be dead soon.

5th Guard.
My wife will be dead soon.

Voice from off stage.
Oi!

3rd Guard.
Something's happening

(Peasant enters carrying the placard, which now reads '1537' he walks across the stage and exits.)

(1st Guard goes off stage and brings back a portrait of Jane Seymour. Alternatively the guard brings back the actress holding a picture frame in front of herself and places her between Guards 2 and 3.)

1st Guard.
Bad news I'm afraid.

2nd Guard.
That's my mum for you. She knows everything.

4th Guard.
Mum's always do.

The Season of The King

3rd Guard.
> I heard Jane Seymour had a little boy before she died.

5th Guard.
> Yes and she named him Edward after me.

4th Guard.
> Your name's not Edward.

5th Guard.
> Yes it is, only spelt differently.

3rd Guard.
> S...I...D.

6th Guard.
> Attention! Make way for the King and the new Queen.

(Peasant enters carrying the placard, which now reads '1540', he walks across the stage and exits.)

(Enter King Henry VIII with Anne of Cleves from stage left, they are not arm in arm, in fact they are a distance apart. A boy plays Anne of Cleves; he is holding a portrait of himself as a beautiful girl.)

Anne of Cleves.
> Your Majesty. I think Mr Holbein painted me beautifully. *(Anne of Cleves points to the portrait she is carrying.)* Do you like the painting?

Henry VIII.
> I think the frame is nice. *(Henry VIII starts pacing up and down the stage and then shouts.)* I want a divorce.

Anne of Cleves.
But, we haven't been married for 5 minutes.

Henry VII.
I don't care.

Anne of Cleves.
All right, as long as you give me a big palace to live in and I can eat my favourite food all day. Chocolate.

Henry VIII.
Anything, to get rid of you madam.

(Henry VIII quickly marches off stage right and Anne of Cleves follows.)

6th Guard.
At ease!

1st Guard.
Oh dear, Anne of Cleves wasn't very pretty.

2nd Guard.
My mum says you shouldn't judge a book by it's cover.

1st Guard.
What does that mean?

2nd Guard.
I don't know. She just says it.

3rd Guard.
Anne of Cleves likes chocolate a lot.

The Season of The King

4th Guard.

You mean she likes a lot of chocolate. I've heard she has it for breakfast, lunch, dinner and even supper. You should see the size of her now.

5th Guard.

My wife likes chocolate.

(Peasant enters carrying the placard, which now reads '1541', he walks across the stage and exits.)

(1st Guard goes off stage and brings back the portrait of Anne of Cleves. Alternatively the guard brings back the actor holding a picture frame in front of himself and places him between Guards 4 and 5.)

6th Guard.

Attention! Make way for the King and the new Queen.

(Enter King Henry VIII with Catherine Howard stage right. They walk across the stage arm in arm.)

Henry VIII.

You are very young and I am getting on a bit.

Catherine Howard.

Your majesty you're not old, you don't look a day over 50.

Henry VIII.

I'm not, I'm 49!

Catherine Howard.

(She giggles nervously.) Oh! Your majesty, you can be any age you like. After all, you are the King.

The Season of The King

Henry VIII.
Of Course I can. And who will Argue, Eh! Eh! *(Laughs.)*

Catherine Howard
(Aside.) Nobody, if they value their life.

(Exit King Henry VIII and Catherine Howard to stage left.)

6th Guard.
At ease! *(The guards relax.)*

4th Guard.
I've seen that Catherine Howard sneaking around the palace.

1st Guard.
I don't blame her. The Kings always in a bad mood.

2nd Guard.
Yes, but my mum says she still has a boyfriend.

3rd Guard.
Your mum's got a boyfriend?

2nd Guard.
No. She says that Catherine Howard's got one.

4th Guard.
But she's married to the king. She's his fifth wife.

2nd Guard.
Exactly!

The Season of The King

1st Guard.
   No she's not. Not any more anyway

4th Guard.
   But, I thought...?

(Peasant enters carrying the placard, which now reads '1542', he walks across the stage and exits.)

(1st Guard goes off stage and brings out Catherine Howard with her head covered; she kneels at the table positioned between Guards 5 and 6 and rests her chin on the top of the table. The cloth is then removed to reveal Catherine Howard's head.)

3rd Guard.
   No wonder he's in a bad mood

5th Guard.
   My wife's got a boyfriend.

4th Guard.
   The king's in a mood because of his bad leg.

1st Guard.
   The King has got the plague.

5th Guard.
   I've got the plague you know. I've had it since I was little.

1st Guard.
   The King doesn't really have the plague, I only said that to trick you.

3rd Guard.
   You always say that everything has happened to you.

The Season of The King

4th Guard.
>The King has a bad leg though. In fact, his legs are covered in ulcers.

5th Guard.
>It's funny you should say that because I've got...

All Guards.
>NO YOU HAVEN'T!

6th Guard.
>Attention! Make way for the King and the new Queen.

(Peasant enters carrying the placard, which now reads '1543', he walks across the stage and exits.)

(Enter King Henry VIII limping, looking quite old, with Catherine Parr from stage left.)

Henry VIII.
>My legs are really hurting today.

Catherine Parr.
>Never mind, we'll put clean bandages on when we get back.

Henry VIII.
>And then I'll get on my horse and go hunting.

Catherine Parr.
Yes, your majesty I'll warn the servants to get the ropes and winch ready. *(Aside to the audience.)* That's the only way they can get him onto the poor horse.

(Exit King Henry VIII and Catherine Parr to stage right.)

The Season of The King

6th Guard.
> At ease! *(The guards relax.)*

1st Guard.
> I don't know how he manages to ride a horse.

3rd Guard.
> I don't know how the horse carries him around.

2nd Guard.
> My mum says you should be kind to animals.

4th Guard.
> Then someone should be kind to your mum.

2nd Guard.
> Hey! There's no need for that.

5th Guard.
> There's no need for my wife!

(Peasant enters carrying the placard, which now reads '1547', he walks across the stage and exits.)

(Enter Town Crier ringing a bell and carrying a large scroll - he reads from the scroll.)

The Town Crier.
> My Lords, Ladies and Gentlemen. The King is Dead.

All.
> The King is Dead. Long live the King.

The Season of The King

6th Guard. Attention! Guards, right turn. Quick march. Left...Right...Left...Right...Left...Left...etc.

(Everybody marches off stage right.)

THE END

Mary I Takes The Throne

The Succession to the Throne after Henry VIII

Cast List:

5 Peasants

Mr. Parsnip ... The Town Crier

Edward VI

Edward Seymour ... Duke of Somerset.

Lady Jane Grey

The Army (as many as required)

Army Sargeant

Servant

Mary Tudor

The Queen's Guard (2 - 4 Guards)

Mary I Takes The Throne

Scene:

Set in the Town Square and a group of peasants are drinking outside an alehouse. Whilst the action takes place, set at the side of the stage we see inside the kings palace.

(Enter the Town Crier Mr. Parsnip.)

Peasant 1.
Who's he?

Peasant 2.
He is Mr. Parsnip the Town Crier. He tells everyone what's going on. It must be time for the news.

Mr. Parsnip.
Oh yez! Oh yez! Oh yez! Here is the 1547 news. The king is dead, long live the king.

Peasant 1.
How can the king live long if he's dead?

Peasant 2.
No the king's not dead. The king is.

Peasant 3.
Eh?

Peasant 2.
The old King is dead.

Peasant 1.
How old was he?

Mary I Takes The Throne

Peasant 2.
Too old.

Peasant 1.
Too old for what.

Peasant 2.
Too old to be alive. Ha, ha, ha, ha!

Peasant 3.
Eh?

Mr. Parsnip.
Don't you peasants know anything? King Henry VIII is dead. So long live the new king.

Peasants.
(All together.) Oh!

Peasant 1..
Who is the new king?

Mr. Parsnip..
Edward VI.

(Enter young Edward VI into his palace and sits on the Throne.)

Peasant 2.
But he's only nine years old.

Peasant 1.
How can he rule the country if he's only nine?

Mary I Takes The Throne

Peasant 2.
His Uncle is going to help him.

(Enter Edward Seymour his uncle and stands behind Edward VI.)

Peasant 3.
My Uncle never helped me.

Peasant 2.
Your uncle isn't a Duke.

Peasant 1.
Duke of what?

Peasant 2.
Edward VI's uncle is Edward Seymour, Duke of Somerset.

Peasant 1..
How do you get to be a duke then?

Peasant 2.
It helps if your sister is the Queen of England.

Peasant 3.
(Acts not at all interested.) Very Interesting. Huh! I haven't even got a sister.

(All the peasants stand around looking bored and drinking.)
(Enter Peasant 4.)

Peasant 4.
Hey! All of you. Have you heard the news?

(He gives Mr. Parsnip a scroll.)

Mary I Takes The Throne

Peasant 1.
What news?

Peasant 2.
(To Mr. Parsnip.) You didn't say anything.

Mr. Parsnip.
I was just about to. Oh yez! Oh yez! Oh yez!

Peasant 4.
Edward VI is poorly.

Mr. Parsnip.
Here is the 1552 news. The king is poorly.

Peasant 4.
He's going to die.

Mr. Parsnip.
He's going to die.

Peasant 4.
And he's written a will...

Mr. Parsnip.
And he's written a will...

Peasant 4.
This gives the Crown to his cousin...

Mr. Parsnip.
I don't have that bit.

Peasant 4.
Lady Jane Grey.

Mr. Parsnip.
(Wanders off stage mumbling.) Is there a page missing, there seems to be some missing here...

Peasant 1.
But, what about his half sister Mary? She's next in line isn't she?

Peasant 2.
Yes but she's a Catholic.

Peasant 1.
So what?

Peasant 2.
Therefore, she'll make everyone else become a Catholic too.

Peasant 1.
Even if they don't want to?

Peasant 2.
Yes.

Peasant 5.
(Enters holding a scroll.) Where's Mr. Parsnip, here's some news for him.

Peasant 1.
He seems to have gone.

Mary I Takes The Throne

Peasant 3.

Give it to me. *(Peasant 5 gives peasant 3 the scroll and exits.)*

Peasant 1.

Can you read?

Peasant 3.

It can't be that difficult. *(He reads.)* Here is the 1553 news. The king is dead. Long live the Queen. *(In the Palace we see Edward VI collapse on his Throne, the guards then remove him. Enter Lady Jane Grey who sits on the Throne.)*

Peasant 4.

So, I was right then! Lady Jane Grey is our new Queen.

(Enter Peasant 5.)

Peasant 5.

Here is the 1553 News.

Peasant 1.

We've just heard that.

Peasant 5.

This is a new bit.

Peasant 2.

It's all happening isn't it.

Peasant 3.

What is? *(Enter the Army with their Sargeant. They march across the stage.)*

Mary I Takes The Throne

Sargeant.

(Shouts.) Left, Right, Left, Right, Left, Left. Get those arms up, keep in step. Come along now look lively. Left, Right, Left, Right, Left, Left.

Peasant 3.

I do love a parade.

Peasant 5.

Lady Jane grey has been arrested. *(Lady Jane Grey is arrested by the Army.)*

Peasant 1..

What for?

Peasant 5.

For being the Queen, I suppose.

Peasant 2.

Dangerous job that.

Peasant 4.

Who had her arrested then? *(The Army marches back across the stage with Lady Jane Grey.)*

Sargeant.

(Shouts.) Left, Right Left, Right Left, Left. Get those arms up, keep in step. Come along now look lively. Left, Right, Left, Right, Left, Left. *(They exit.)*

Peasant 5.

The Army.

Mary I Takes The Throne

Peasant 2.
But who ordered the Army?

Peasant 5.
Oh I see what you mean. Mary Tudor. She has declared herself Queen. *(Enter Mary I sits on the throne.)*

Peasants 1 and 4.
Uh Oh!

Peasant 5.
Everyone MUST now become a Roman Catholic, and go to Mass on Sundays.

Peasant 1..
Do you know I've always wanted to be a Catholic.

Peasant 2.
I'd like to but I go to the alehouse on Sundays.

Peasant 1.
You'll be on your own then. *(Exits.)*

Peasant 3.
It'll make a nice change; I haven't seen our Priest for years.

Peasant 2.
You're probably right, the alehouse will be shut anyway.

Peasant 4.
Actually chaps, I'm already a Catholic, but I've been keeping it a secret. In case, well you know!

Mary I Takes The Throne

Peasant 5.
Well, I don't want to but I suppose I'll have to. After all I've got a wife and children to support.

(Enter Peasant 1 with another scroll.)

Peasant 5.
(Takes scroll.) What's this? More news.

Peasant 1.
No. More of the same I'm afraid.

Peasant 5.
(Reads.) Anyone who refuses to become Catholic will be burnt alive.

Peasant 2.
That's a bit strong.

Peasant 4.
She is the Queen; She can do, as she likes.

(Enter Mr. Parsnip.)

Mr. Parsnip..
Have I missed anything?
(Enter a Servant of the Queen.)

Servant.
Here comes the Queen, get out of the way, clear the road, she's coming, she's actually only just around the corner she'll be here in a minute, soon, soon, I promise, a moment longer, get ready, prepare to be astonished. Ladies and gentlemen, the Queen. *(Pause.)* She's nearly here, won't be a minute, any second now....

Mary I Takes The Throne

Peasants.
Shut up!

(Enter Queen Mary I with her two guards and everybody bows.)

Mary I.
Stand up if you're a Catholic. *(Everyone stays still except Mr. Parsnip who stands up.)* Arrest him.

Mr. Parsnip.
Have I missed something? Will someone tell me what's going on?

Mary I.
Take him to the stake.

(Mr. Parsnip is arrested by the Queen's guards, tied up, and placed on the bonfire.)

Mr. Parsnip.
I don't like steak. I'm a vegetarian. Even my name is a vegetable.

Peasant 1.
I do like a nice bonfire.

Peasant 2.
It is getting a bit cold, now that you mention it.

Mary I.
This is what happens if you won't change your religion.

(Exit Mary I and her guards set light to the bonfire.)

Mr. Parsnip.
I'll change if you want me to!

Mary I Takes The Throne

Peasant 4.
Too late mate, she's gone.

Peasant 5.
I do like a nice roasted parsnip.

Mr. Parsnip.
Very funny.

(Mr. Parsnip coughs and splutters and tries desperately to blow out the fire, but finally he dies. Exit the Guards and Peasants)

THE END

A Husband For The Queen

The young Queen Elizabeth I is told to marry.

Cast list:

Sir William Cecil

Queen Elizabeth I

Sir Francis Bacon

Ladies in waiting

Lord Walshingham

Servants

Lord Throgmorton

Cooks (two)

Earl Dudley

Muttering Ministers (as many as required.)

Duke D'Alencon

Prince Erik of Sweden

Archduke Charles of Austria

A Husband For The Queen

Scene:
Inside the Houses of Parliament. The ministers are discussing the new Queen of England, Elizabeth I.

Cecil.
Once again gentlemen, we have a Queen to rule over us.

Bacon.
And a very good Queen she will be too.

Cecil.
Of course, of course.

Muttering Ministers.
Hear, hear!

Cecil.
But she is still a woman.

Throgmorton.
A woman alone has never ruled England.

Walshingham.
What about Boudicca.

Muttering Ministers.
Who?

Walshingham.
Never mind. Umm...Lady Jane Grey never married. Cecil. But she only ruled for nine days, and anyway she was never crowned.

A Husband For The Queen

Bacon.
She was married you know Cecil.

Cecil.
Who to?

Bacon.
Lord Guildford Dudley. He had his head chopped off with her.

Throgmorton.
Aah that's nice! *(Everybody looks at Throgmorton.)* Well it is nice, doing things together. Very romantic.

Walshingham.
What about our late Queen Mary...

Muttering Ministers.
God Bless Her.

Walshingham.
She wasn't married.

Bacon.
Sorry!

Walshingham.
Don't tell me.

Bacon.
Yes. She was married to Phillip II of Spain.

Throgmorton.
You see, nobody listens to me. England has never been ruled by a woman alone.

A Husband For The Queen

Cecil.
Queen, Throgmorton.

Throgmorton.
There wasn't a Queen called Throgmorton. My name is Throgmorton and I should know.

Dudley.
Something must be done.

Muttering Ministers.
(They start pacing up and down and muttering several times.) Something must be done, something must be done.

Dudley.
I have it.

Cecil.
But what!

Dudley.
She will have to get married!

(The Muttering Ministers make an audible intake of breath, there is a pause then they all start talking at once.)

Muttering Ministers.
Not to me. I'm already married. How old is she? I'd make a good king. I promised my mum I'd never get married Is there money in it? Would you have to kiss her? Etc.

Dudley.
Not to any of you.

A Husband For The Queen

Muttering Ministers.
Phew! *(Exit Muttering Ministers.)*

Cecil.
Of course, she'll have to marry a Prince.

Bacon.
Or a duke.

Throgmorton.
At the very least!

Walshingham.
I, Lord Walshingham will find her a husband. We will have to start a search.

Bacon.
What do you mean "We"?

Dudley.
When I said that Her Majesty wouldn't marry any of you. What I meant was, that she'll marry me.

Cecil.
Don't be silly, she couldn't marry you. Everyone! We'll have to go to France. *(All the ministers, except Dudley, march to the side of the stage where a Frenchman, The Duke D'Alencon, has made his entrance.)*

Duke.
(With a French accent) 'Allo. 'Ow are you?

Throgmorton.
We're very pleased to meet you.

A Husband For The Queen

Walshingham.
Are you a Duke?

Duke.
Oui! I am the Duke D'Alencon.

Bacon.
Oh good. Would you like to get married?

Duke.
But, I don't even know you.

Bacon.
No, not to me you twit. My name is Bacon, How do you do. *(The Duke Laughs.)*

Bacon.
What's so funny?

Duke.
Bacon is of the pig, yes?

Bacon.
Really!

Cecil.
Would you marry our Queen?

Throgmorton.
Elizabeth the First.

Walshingham.
Of England.

A Husband For The Queen

Duke.
Aah, but of course.

Walshingham.
We'll make an appointment.

(All the ministers return to centre stage, where Dudley is waiting.)

Cecil.
That's one suitor sorted.

Dudley.
She will marry me you know, I've got loads of money.

Walshingham.
It's just not going to happen Dudley.

Bacon.
Let's go to Sweden.

(They all go to Sweden, which is on the other side of the stage, where Prince Erik has made his entrance. Dudley waits centre stage.)

Throgmorton.
It's Prince Erik of Sweden isn't it?

Prince Erik.
(With a Swedish accent.) Is it? Where?

Throgmorton.
No. You are Prince Erik. Aren't you?

A Husband For The Queen

Prince Erik.
Yes, yes, yes. Just my little joke. What do you want?

Cecil.
We would like you to marry our Queen.

Prince Erik.
Oh, yes please, she is very rich, er... beautiful, is she not?

Walshingham.
Most certainly.

Prince Erik.
Very well then.

Bacon.
We'll make an appointment.

(All ministers return centre stage, where Dudley is waiting.)

Walshingham.
That's two suitors sorted.

Dudley.
Look I've told you, I have loads of land, she'll want to marry me.

Throgmorton.
But she can't, and that's final.

Cecil.
I say we go to Austria.

A Husband For The Queen

(All ministers, except Dudley, set of for Austria, which is in another area of the stage. The Archduke Charles makes his entrance.)

Archduke.
(With a Austrian accent.) I knew you'd come, you want me to marry Queen Elizabeth. Wait there, I'll pack a bag.

Bacon.
My dear Archduke Charles, we can't wait, but we will make an appointment.

(All ministers return centre stage, where Dudley is waiting.)

Throgmorton.
There, that's three suitors. That should be enough.

Dudley.
Why can't the Queen marry me?

All Ministers.
(They look at Dudley.) Because you're already married.

(Exit all ministers.)

Scene II.
Queen Elizabeth I is in her palace surrounded by Ladies in waiting and servants. The Ladies are all fussing around her, fixing her hair, checking her make up, tidying her dress etc.

Elizabeth 1.
I'm fed up; I've been wearing this old dress all day. I want to change. Girl, fetch me my new gold dress.

A Husband For The Queen

Lady 1.
   (Curtseys.) Yes your Majesty. *(She goes toward the door.)*

Elizabeth 1.
   Girl.

Lady 1.
   (Returns to the Queen.) Yes, your Majesty.

Elizabeth 1.
   I have changed my mind. Get the red one.

Lady 1.
   (Curtseys.) Yes, your Majesty. *(She goes toward the door.)*

Elizabeth 1.
   Girl.

Lady 1.
   (Returns to the Queen.) Yes, your Majesty.

Elizabeth 1.
   I have changed my mind. Get the silver one.

Lady 1.
   (Curtseys.) Yes, your Majesty. *(She goes toward the door.)*

Elizabeth 1.
   Girl.

Lady 1.
   (Returns to the Queen.) Yes, your Majesty

Elizabeth 1.
   I have changed my mind. I like this one. You, servant.

A Husband For The Queen

Servant 1.
(Curtseys or bows.) Yes, your Majesty

Elizabeth 1.
Is everyone ready for the feast?

Servant 1.
They are, your Majesty.

Elizabeth 1.
Cooks! *(Enter the cooks.)*

Cooks.
(They say everything together.) Here we are, your Majesty.

Elizabeth 1.
What will we have to eat?

Cooks.
Roast Beef, Stuffed Peacock, Swan's neck, Quail's eggs, Wild Boar, Whale steak...

Elizabeth 1.
... And to drink?

Cooks.
In between every course, there will be ale, wine and mead.

Elizabeth.1.
Good. *(There is a knock on the door.)* Servant, see who is at the door.

Servant 2.
Yes your majesty. *(The servant goes to the door and opens it.)* Who is it?

A Husband For The Queen

Walshingham.
(Enters.) Walshingham.

Cecil.
(Enters.) Cecil.

Throgmorton.
(Enters.) Throgmorton.

Dudley.
(Enters.) Dudley.

Bacon.
(Enters.) Bacon. *(The servant laughs.)*

Bacon.
What are you laughing at?

Servant 2.
Nothing sir.

Elizabeth 1.
Who is it?

Servant 2.
Walshingham, Cecil, Throgmorton, Dudley and Bacon, your Majesty. *(The ministers bow and Queen Elizabeth laughs.)*

Bacon.
Why does everyone laugh at my name?

Elizabeth 1.
Because it's funny, my little pork pie. *(Everyone except Bacon laughs.)*

A Husband For The Queen

Walshingham.
Your Majesty, we are here on serious business.

Elizabeth 1.
Oh yes. What's that then?

Throgmorton.
We have a list of three men who would like to marry you. *(He hands the Queen a list.)*

Elizabeth 1.
Ah! This should be fun. Where are they?

Cecil.
They are waiting without. *(Gestures to the door.)*

Elizabeth 1.
Without what? Ha! Ha! Ha! Ha!

Dudley.
They're outside Ma'am.

Elizabeth 1.
I knew that. Well? Show them in. First the Duke D'Alencon.

Servant 1.
Call the Duke D'Alencon.

Servant 2.
Call the Duke D'Alencon.

Servant 3.
Call the Duke D'Alencon. *(Enter Duke D'Alencon.)*

A Husband For The Queen

Duke.
It is I, Duke D'Alencon. Your most Gracious Majesty, will you marry me?

Elizabeth 1.
How far have you come, to ask me?

Duke.
All the way from France.

Elizabeth 1.
You'll just have to go right back there. No!

(Exit the Duke D'Alencon.)

Elizabeth 1.
Next, I'll see Prince Erik of Sweden.

Servant 1.
Call Prince Erik of Sweden.

Servant 2.
Call Prince Erik of Sweden.

Servant 3.
Call Prince Erik of Sweden.

Prince Erik.
(Enter the Prince.) It is I, Prince Erik. Your most Gracious Majesty, will you marry me?

Elizabeth 1.
How far have you come, to ask me?

A Husband For The Queen

Prince Erik.
All the way from Sweden.

Elizabeth 1.
Is it cold there?

Prince Erik.
Why yes Madam.

Elizabeth 1.
Then use a warming pan. Next! *(Exit he Prince.)* I'll see Archduke Charles.

Servant 1.
Call Archduke Charles.

Servant 2.
Call Archduke Charles.

Servant 3.
Call Archduke Charles.

Archduke Charles.
(Enter the Archduke.) I have changed my mind. I do not want to get married.

Lady in waiting.
Are you sure?

Archduke Charles.
(Looks at the Lady in waiting, smiles.) Well for you, I will change my mind again. *(They exit together.)*

Elizabeth 1.
Ladies and gentlemen, that seems to be that.

Dudley.
(Suspiciously.) Your Majesty, I'm not married any more. My wife seems to have mysteriously, accidentally, fallen downstairs and died suddenly.

Elizabeth 1.
I have decided that I will never marry. I am married to England.

Dudley.
Drat! I needn't have bothered.

(Exit the Queen, Ministers and servants of the court.)

THE END